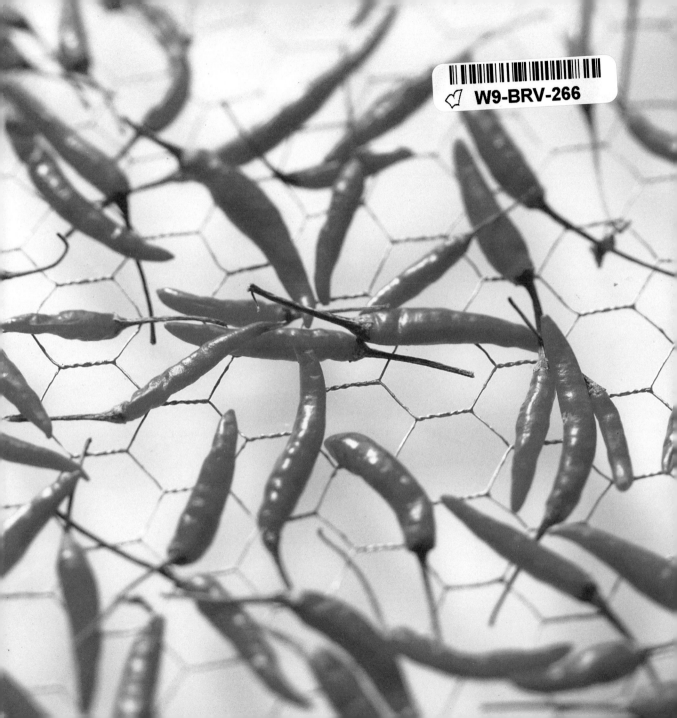

flavoring with
Chiles

flavoring with
Chiles

Clare Gordon-Smith

photography by

James Merrell

RYLAND
PETERS
& SMALL

Art Director **Jacqui Small**

Art Editor **Penny Stock**

Design Assistant **Mark Latter**

Editor **Elsa Petersen-Schepelern**

Photography **James Merrell**

Food Stylist **Clare Gordon-Smith**

Stylist **Sue Skeen**

Production Consultant **Vincent Smith**

Our thanks to Christine Walsh, Ian Bartlett, Dodie Miller of The Cool Chilli Company, Mohammad Hanif of J.H. Halal and Sally Everett of Food Link (Eastern) Ltd.

First published in the USA in 1996
This edition published in 2000 by
Ryland Peters & Small
Cavendish House
51–55 Mortimer Street, London W1N 7TD

10 9 8 7 6 5 4 3 2 1

Text © Clare Gordon-Smith 1996
Design © Ryland Peters & Small 1996

Printed and bound in China by Toppan Printing Co.

ISBN 1-84172-064-X

A CIP catalog record for this book is available from the Library of Congress.

Notes:
Ovens should be preheated to the specified temperature. If using a convection oven, adjust time and temperature according to the manufacturer's instructions.

Chiles, native to Central and South America, have been enthusiastically adopted by cooks in Europe, Africa, the Middle East, India, and Southeast Asia, as well as the Americas. Hundreds of different varieties have been identified. Commercially available fresh chiles include, from left, the **Anaheim**, green when unripe and red when ripe, which is widely used in the canning industry and is also available fresh. The fiery yellow and red **Jamaican Scotch bonnets** are used in West Indian curries, especially the delectable jerk sauces. Their fruity, smoky flavor is delicious with tropical fruit. The smaller red Jamaican hot chile is a close relation. Red and green **Thai** and other **Asian** chiles are blazing hot, with a clear fiery taste. Red and green **serrano** chiles are especially suited to roasting, or used fresh in salsas. Yellow, red, and orange **habaneros**, closely related to bonnets, are fruity and searingly hot. The mild pale yellow **caribe** can be used raw in salads. The green **Korean** chile is as hot as its Thai cousin. Large red and green **New Mexico** chiles, close cousins to the Anaheims, are mild, fleshy, and sweet, mostly roasted and used in sauces, salsas, and stews.

the flavors of

Chiles

Guajillo
A mild chile said to taste of "green tea." Used in salsas and sauces.

Pasado
(not shown)
Roasted and peeled—this chile tastes of apple and citrus.

Choricero
(not shown)
A very sweet, mild chile from Spain. This one is large enough to take a filling, and can also be added to soups, casseroles, and sauces.

Mulato
Sweet and fruity with a smoky taste—this chile is said to taste of licorice. The mulato can be filled, or cut into strips and used in Mexican molés.

Cascabel (The Little Rattle)
Pretty little chiles that have a nutty taste, thick flesh, and medium heat. Soak them first then use in sauces, soups, casseroles, and salsas.

New Mexico Red
A very popular large red chile with an earthy, fruity, flavor, that's good in red sauces.

Tepin Flea Chile
A small, wild, hand-picked chile—very hot indeed. Said to taste also of corn and nuts, these chiles are usually crushed onto cooked dishes, or used in chile oils and vinegars.

There are dozens of different kinds of **chiles,** and some have become identified with the cuisine of particular countries. For instance the **fiery** serranos and jalapeños are widely used in Mexico and the United States. Scotch bonnets are identified with Caribbean cooking, while cayenne types are the most popular in India and the Pacific Rim nations of Asia. Native to Mexico, the chile has been used in cooking for 7,000 years. It was first discovered and taken to Europe after Christopher Columbus's voyage to the New World in 1492, then introduced to Europe, Asia, and Africa by the Spaniards and Portuguese.

Nyora
(not shown)
Another Spanish chile with a good, sweet, fruity flavor, suitable for use in soups, casseroles, and salsas.

Bird's Eye
An orange chile from East Africa. This chile is perfect for soups, casseroles, chile oils, vinegars, and for Portuguese piri piri sauce.

Guindilla
(not shown)
A sweet Spanish chile that's medium hot. It can be used in a wide range of dishes to give extra pizzazz.

Pasilla (The Little Raisin)
Used to flavor fish dishes and Mexican molés. Medium hot, it tastes of berries and licorice.

Habanero
The hottest chile of all—use in fish stews and curries. It's also good in salsas.

Chipotle
(not shown)
A very versatile, but rather hot chile with a smoky, nutty flavor.

Ancho
(not shown)
Sweet, mild, and fruity, this chile can be filled, sliced, or added to sauces, such as molés. If cooking with a filling, remove the seeds but leave the stems intact.

The chemical that produces a chile's fiery taste is capsaicin. The major part of the **spicy** heat is in the seeds and membranes, and these should be removed before cooking. When using whole dried chiles, pour over boiling water, soak for about 20 minutes, then remove the stem and seeds.

For a nutty taste, dry roast the dried chiles before using, taking care not to burn them—burnt chiles taste bitter. Capsaicin is not water soluble, so if your chile is too hot, don't drink water, beer, or wine—milk or yogurt will quell the fires.

Appetizers

Thai clear soup
with sweet and sour chile

A clear Thai soup with chile as the main flavoring ingredient. Good quality, flavorful chicken stock is also vital, but if you haven't time to make your own, many supermarkets now sell freshly made stocks.

If using the Chinese mushrooms, place them in a small bowl, cover with boiling water and soak for 30 minutes.

Place the stock, garlic, ginger, rice vinegar, and brown sugar in a pan and heat, stirring constantly, until gently simmering.

Add the chicken, scallions, lemongrass, red chile, and Chinese mushrooms, if using, and continue to simmer for 15 to 20 minutes.

Taste and adjust the seasoning, remove the lemongrass, then serve the soup, garnished with fresh cilantro leaves.

3 Chinese mushrooms, (optional)

3¾ cups chicken stock

2 garlic cloves

1 tablespoon sliced pickled ginger

1½ tablespoons rice vinegar

2 teaspoons soft brown sugar

1 chicken breast, very finely sliced

4 scallions, sliced

2 stalks lemongrass, halved lengthwise

1 red Thai chile

salt and freshly ground black pepper

fresh cilantro leaves, to garnish

Serves 4

Steamed mussels
in a red chile broth

Use the large, dried, red New Mexico chiles illustrated on page 8. They are available by mail order if you have difficulty finding them in specialist shops, or you could substitute one small dried red chile (much hotter than the New Mexico version). Mussels are naturally inclined to be salty, so take care when seasoning this recipe.

Roast the garlic and tomatoes in a preheated oven at 300°F for 1 hour.
To make the broth, soak the chiles in the stock and water for about 1 hour until softened and limp. Puree in a blender and set aside.
Heat 1 tablespoon of the olive oil in a pan and sauté the garlic and tomato until reheated. Add the mussels, stir in the broth, cover, and steam for about 5 to 7 minutes until the mussels have opened. Discard any that remain closed.
Taste and adjust the seasoning.
Stir in the cream, if using, and serve immediately with a sprinkling of ground paprika, accompanied by toasted sourdough bread.

2 garlic cloves

4 red tomatoes, sliced

2 dried red New Mexico chiles, seeded

1¼ cups fish stock

⅔ cup water

2 tablespoons olive oil

2 lb. mussels, scrubbed and debearded

⅔ cup light cream (optional)

salt and freshly ground black pepper

ground paprika, to serve

Serves 4

a **hot and smoky** marriage of New Mexic

hiles and shellfish

Scallop chowder
with Jamaican Scotch bonnets

Chowders are an American contribution to the world's culinary repertoire, and the sweet scallop flavor really comes through in this version. Jamaican Scotch bonnet chiles are brilliant red or sunny yellow—and very fiery! If you can't find Scotch bonnets, use their close cousins, habaneros, or any other hot, red, fresh chiles—bonnets are quite large, so you'll need several smaller ones. Jamaicans cook them whole in soups and remove them before serving. The result is an amazing spicy fruity flavor.

Place the scallops in a bowl, sprinkle with lime juice and set aside for a few minutes.

Brown the bacon in a large, heavy-based skillet and drain off any excess fat. Add the olive oil and, when hot, add the shallot, celery, garlic, and sliced Scotch bonnet. Sauté gently for a few minutes until lightly browned, stir in the tomatoes and sherry, then bring to a boil to burn off the alcohol.

Dice the potatoes and stir into the pan, then add the herbs and fish stock.

Reserve a few scallops for garnish then chop the remainder and add to the chowder.

Bring to a boil, simmer for 20 minutes, then taste and adjust the seasoning.

Garnish with parsley and the reserved, sliced scallops. Serve with toasted cornbread.

8 oz. scallops

3 tablespoons lime juice

2 slices bacon, chopped

1 tablespoon olive oil

1 shallot, finely chopped

2 celery stalks,
finely chopped

2 garlic cloves, crushed

½ red Jamaican
Scotch bonnet chile,
seeded and sliced

3 tomatoes, peeled,
seeded, and chopped

2 tablespoons
dry sherry

1 lb. potatoes

2 bay leaves

1 bunch of fresh, flat-
leaf parsley, chopped,
plus 4 tablespoons,
to serve

2 cups fish stock

salt and pepper

Serves 4

Roasted chile soup
with yellow and red bell peppers

This vibrantly colored soup has a bright zip
of chile coming through the tomato and
pepper flavors. Serve hot or chilled.

Place the red and yellow bell peppers and the red
chile under a very hot broiler and roast on all sides
until the skins are blackened and blistered. Place in
plastic wrap and leave to steam for 5 to 7 minutes.
Pull out the stems and seeds, scrape off the skin and
discard. Slice the flesh into strips and reserve the
yellow bell pepper for garnish.
Heat the oil in a large saucepan, add the shallot or
onion, the tomatoes, chile, and red bell peppers,
replace the lid and cook the vegetables for about
5 minutes until softened. Stir in the stock and
seasoning and simmer for 20 minutes until all the
vegetables are tender. Place in a blender or food
processor and puree until smooth.
Reheat, taste, and adjust the seasoning.
Serve garnished with the strips of yellow bell pepper
and a drizzle of chile oil, accompanied by the
croutons and crème fraîche.

2 red bell peppers

1 red serrano
chile, roasted

1 tablespoon sunflower
oil, or other mild oil

1 shallot or small onion,
finely chopped

1 lb. ripe red plum
tomatoes, peeled
and seeded

2 cups vegetable stock

salt and freshly
ground black pepper

to serve

1 yellow bell pepper

croutons

4 tablespoons
crème fraîche

chile oil, to taste

Serves 4

Chile aioli
with char-grilled vegetables

Aioli is the wonderful garlic mayonnaise from Provence, served with steamed vegetables and salt cod or other poached fish. To save time, you could also make it by adding the chile, garlic, and breadcrumbs to good quality store-bought mayonnaise.

a selection of vegetables, such as baby artichokes, asparagus, fennel, leeks, or bell peppers

sea salt

olive oil, for brushing

chile aioli

1 red habanero chile

2 garlic cloves, crushed

egg yolk substitute, equivalent to 2 egg yolks

3 tablespoons fresh white breadcrumbs

4 tablespoons white wine vinegar

1 cup olive oil

1 tablespoon boiling water (optional)

pinch of salt

Serves 4

To prepare the vegetables, first par-boil the artichokes, then drain. Brush all the vegetables with olive oil, sprinkle with sea salt and cook under a very hot broiler, or on a grill pan on top of the stove, until nicely browned.

To make the aïoli, first place the chile under the broiler and roast until the skin is blistered and browned. Pull out the stem and seeds, and mash the flesh. Place the garlic, egg yolk substitute, breadcrumbs, mashed chile, salt, and vinegar in a food processor and puree to a paste. With the motor still running, pour in the olive oil in a thin stream until the mixture forms a thick sauce. Thin out with a little boiling water if necessary.

Serve as a dip with the roasted vegetables or, as an alternative, with raw crudités.

Chile-filled squid
with arugula and chile oil

Baby squid are delicious filled with a mixture of sweet brióche crumbs, chiles, and serrano ham—a great appetizer, and wonderful as a main course for lunch, served with rice or couscous. If you don't have a stove-top grill pan, you could also cook the squid on a barbecue, or roast in a hot oven at 400°F for 10 minutes.

To make the filling, melt the butter in a skillet and, when sizzling, add the brióche crumbs and sauté until golden. Remove from the skillet, place in a bowl and mix with the remaining filling ingredients. To prepare the squid, gently pull the body away from the head and tentacles, then cut off the tentacles and reserve. Rinse out the bodies and discard the transparent quill and the head. Place the filling mixture loosely in each squid and fasten shut using soaked wooden cocktail sticks. Brush the squid with olive oil and season with salt and freshly ground black pepper. Heat an oiled cast-iron grill pan on top of the stove, and sear the squid (with tentacles) for 5 minutes on each side. To serve, arrange the arugula or mustard leaves on serving plates, and place the squid on top. Drizzle with chile oil and serve immediately.

8 squid

olive oil, for brushing

chile filling

2 tablespoons butter

1 cup briôche crumbs

1 tablespoon
finely chopped
fresh cilantro leaves

1 garlic clove, crushed

1 green habanero chile,
finely chopped

2 slices serrano or
Parma ham, finely
chopped

grated rind and
juice of 1 lime

salt and freshly
ground black pepper

to serve

8 oz. arugula or
mustard leaves

chile oil

Serves 4

an easy, stunning dish with a **mild** chile flavor

Crab pillows
with chile dipping sauce

A delicious appetizer. You can use store-bought chile dipping sauce or make your own. Seed and chop 1 red chile, then mix with 6 tablespoons rice vinegar and 2 tablespoons ketchup.

6 sheets ricepaper

oil, for deep-frying

½ cup chile dipping sauce (see introduction)

crab filling

2 green Thai chiles

3 scallions

1 bunch of cilantro

4 Chinese mushrooms

2 oz. transparent noodles

6 oz. white crabmeat

2 teaspoons soy sauce

1 tablespoon fish sauce

Serves 4

Mix all the chile dipping sauce ingredients together, place in a small bowl and set aside.
To make the filling, seed and chop the chiles, then finely chop the scallions and cilantro.
Soak the mushrooms and noodles separately in warm water for 10 minutes, then drain.
Mix all the filling ingredients together.
To make the pillows, soak the ricepaper in warm water until soft, spoon a small amount of filling into the center of each sheet and fold into pillows.
Cover with a damp cloth to prevent them drying out.
Heat the oil in a saucepan and deep-fry the pillows for a few minutes, until pale gold and crispy.
Serve immediately with the chile dipping sauce.

a wonderful **partnership**—chiles and crab

are one of the great combinations

Crab cakes
with sweet red pepper sauce

Crab cakes make great appetizers—and are excellent party food. Chile and crab seem just made for each other! Use one small red chile if you can't find jalapeños.

Mix the breadcrumbs, egg, crabmeat, jalapeño chiles, cilantro, salt, and freshly ground black pepper in a bowl. Cover and set aside.

To make the sauce, peel the bell peppers with a vegetable peeler, cut in half, seed, and roughly chop. Seed and chop the red chile. Place in a saucepan with the shallots, herbs, garlic, peppercorns, and tomato. Add the stock, bring to a boil, and simmer until soft. Add the white vermouth and vinegar, bring to a boil and reduce for 3 to 4 minutes. Place in a blender or food processor and puree until smooth. Return to the pan, reheat and simmer gently until ready to serve.

To cook the crab cakes, heat the oil in a large skillet until hot but not smoking. Add spoonfuls of the mixture and cook for a few minutes on each side until golden. Drain on paper towels.

Serve with the hot red pepper sauce. A few green salad leaves would be a suitable accompaniment.

2 cups dried breadcrumbs

1 egg, lightly beaten

1 lb. crabmeat

1–2 jalapeño chiles, seeded and diced

1 bunch of cilantro, roughly chopped

peanut oil, for frying

salt and pepper

red pepper sauce

2 red bell peppers

1 small red chile

2 shallots, sliced

1 sprig of thyme

1 garlic clove, crushed

10 black peppercorns

1 plum tomato, sliced

1 cup vegetable stock

4 tablespoons white vermouth

1 tablespoon white wine vinegar

Serves 4

Entrees

Thai seafood curry
with cilantro and coconut milk

Thai fish curries taste clean and fresh, and
are absolutely packed with spicy flavor. It's
important not to overcook the seafood, so
remove it from the broth as soon as it is
cooked, then reheat just before serving.

Pour the coconut milk into a pan, add the chiles and
lemongrass, and bring to a boil.
Add the mussels and remove as soon as they open.
Add the pieces of fish and the tiger shrimp and
poach gently until the shrimp change color and the
fish becomes opaque. Remove from the pan and set
aside with the mussels. Return the coconut milk to a
boil and reduce by half. Return the seafood to the
pan and reheat, then serve with fragrant Thai rice or
pasta, sprinkled with torn cilantro leaves.

1 cup coconut milk

1 red Thai chile, seeded
and sliced

1 green Thai chile,
seeded and sliced

2 stalks of lemongrass,
cut in half lengthwise

1 lb. mussels, scrubbed
and debearded

1 lb. monkfish, cod, or
similar firm-fleshed fish

1 lb. uncooked
tiger shrimp, shelled
and deveined

leaves from 1 bunch
of cilantro, torn

fragrant Thai rice,
or pasta, to serve

Serves 4

Shrimp brochettes
with chile, papaya, and mango salsa

You can adapt this recipe for the barbecue—
the woodsmoke adds a marvelous depth of
flavor. For extra flavor, always cook the
shrimp with their shells on.

To make the salsa, mix the ingredients together in a
small container, cover, and chill for up to 6 hours.
Place the shrimp in a bowl, sprinkle over the chile oil
and the juice of 2 limes. Marinate for 1 to 2 hours.
Soak 4 wooden skewers in water for 30 minutes.
Place a wedge of red onion on each skewer, then
thread on the shrimp, followed by a slice of lime.
Brush with the marinade, sprinkle with sea salt,
then cook under a preheated broiler for a few
minutes on each side.
Garnish with wedges of lime and onion, the sliced
chile, and torn cilantro leaves.
Serve with rice, pita bread, or salad, with the salsa
spooned over or served separately.

salsas are thick and chunky sauces—ideal made wit

fresh fruit. This one is also wonderf

...hopped

...ade with grapes.

24 unpeeled shrimp

1 teaspoon chile oil

juice of 4 limes,
1 lime, sliced, and
1 lime, quartered

1 large red onion,
cut into 8 wedges

sea salt

chile, papaya, and mango salsa

1 large, ripe mango,
peeled, seeded
and diced

1 ripe papaya, about
8 oz., peeled, seeded
and diced

1 tablespoon
balsamic vinegar

1 tablespoon chopped
fresh red chiles

salt and freshly
ground black pepper

to serve

1 fresh red chile, sliced

fresh cilantro leaves

Serves 4

Pork tenderloin
with red apple chile chutney

This sparkling fresh chutney of apples and chile, with just a hint of vinegar, is a terrific new approach to the traditional applesauce. If you can't find habanero chiles, use a Scotch bonnet or two small Asian chiles.

Mix the marinade ingredients together. Trim any fat from the pork, place the meat in a flat dish, pour over the marinade, cover with plastic wrap, and set aside in the refrigerator for 1 hour, or overnight. When ready to cook, remove the meat from the marinade, pat dry, and place in a roasting pan. Roast in a preheated oven at 400°F for 20 to 30 minutes, until well cooked. Remove from the pan and set aside to rest in a warm place for about 5 minutes. Meanwhile, to make the chutney, heat the oil in a shallow skillet, add the shallot and cook until soft and golden. Chop the apple, add to the pan, and stir. Add the remaining ingredients, together with the marinade juices, stir well, bring to a boil and simmer for 15 minutes. Cut the pork into slices and serve with the apple and chile chutney. Pappardelle or other egg pasta tossed in extra-virgin olive oil and the green chile paste on page 61 are suitable accompaniments.

1 lb. pork fillet

orange marinade

grated rind and juice of 2 oranges

1 teaspoon lemon juice

1 garlic clove, crushed

1 teaspoon soy sauce

1–2 teaspoons chili powder

1 teaspoon soft brown sugar

red apple chile chutney

2 teaspoons chile oil

1 shallot or small onion, finely chopped

2 red apples

1 red habanero chile, seeded and chopped

2 tablespoons sherry vinegar

pinch of sea salt

Serves 4

Garlic ginger chicken
with raspberry harissa

A recipe created by talented London designer Dinny Hall—and very stylish it is too! Cook in a roasting pan, or in a chicken brick, with enough chicken stock added to fill the brick to about 2 inches deep.

Pierce the skin of the chicken at regular intervals and insert small pieces of garlic and ginger. Brush the chicken with a little chile oil and place in a roasting pan (or soaked chicken brick with chicken stock added). Cook in a preheated oven at 400°F for about 1½ hours, until tender.

To make the harissa, heat the olive oil, add the sliced onions, and sauté until golden. Add the garlic, mustard seeds, bay leaf, chili powder, salt, and vinegar and cook gently until the mixture is soft and golden. Add the tomatoes and raspberries, bring to a boil and simmer on a low heat for 1 hour. Remove and discard the bay leaf, pour the mixture into a blender or food processor, and puree until smooth.

Remove the chicken from the oven and serve accompanied by the harissa and couscous, spiced with chile oil, cinnamon, garlic, and vanilla.

1 chicken, about 4 lb.,
free-range if available

2 garlic cloves,
finely sliced

1 inch fresh ginger,
peeled and sliced

2 teaspoons chile oil

chicken stock
(see method)

couscous, to serve

raspberry harissa

2 tablespoons olive oil

2 red onions,
finely chopped

1 garlic clove, crushed

1 teaspoon mustard
seeds, lightly crushed

1 bay leaf

1 teaspoon chili
powder, or to taste

1 tablespoon vinegar

8 oz. tomatoes, peeled

1½ cups raspberries

salt

Serves 4

Chicken and chorizo
in a chile and orange sauce

An easy, spicy, one-pot dish. Pretty red
Camargue rice from France has a nutty
taste, but you could use basmati instead.

1 lb. potatoes

4 plum tomatoes

2 tablespoons olive oil

8 oz. baby onions

2 whole garlic cloves

4 chicken breasts

2 chorizo sausages

1–2 tablespoons hot
chile paste or harissa

pinch of chili powder

3 tablespoons sherry

grated rind and juice
of 1 large orange

salt and pepper

to serve

toasted cumin seeds

sour cream

Serves 4

Peel the potatoes and cut into chunks, then peel and
chop the tomatoes. Heat the oil in a large skillet, add
the potatoes and onions and sauté for 10 minutes,
then add the garlic and cook until golden.
Cut the chicken breasts into 2-inch pieces, thickly
slice the chorizos, then stir into the potato and onion
mixture. Stir in the tomatoes, harissa, sherry, orange
rind, and juice. Taste and adjust the seasoning, then
simmer for 15 minutes, until the chicken is tender.
Sprinkle with toasted cumin seeds and serve with a
dollop of sour cream.
Steamed red Camargue rice, and a crisp green salad
are suitable accompaniments.

Marinated duck breasts
with orange salsa and sherry sauce

A Pan-Pacific recipe, combining the culinary traditions of Asia and Mexico. The chile flavoring in the marinade comes from Tabasco sauce, made in Louisiana since the middle of last century, from chiles which originated in the Mexican state of Tabasco.

Score the duck skin in a criss-cross pattern to help the fat melt off during cooking. Place the breasts in a roasting pan with the skin side up.

Mix the marinade ingredients together, pour over the duck and set aside for at least 30 minutes. Meanwhile, to make the salsa, mix all the ingredients together and chill until ready to serve.

Place the duck breasts and marinade in a roasting pan and cook in a preheated oven at 400°F for about 20 minutes or until just pink. Remove the breasts and set aside in a warm place.

Drain the fat from the roasting pan, add the sherry, bring to a boil to remove the alcohol, then stir in the stock and simmer for 5 minutes.

Slice the duck breasts and serve with the sherry sauce and orange salsa, accompanied by stir-fried cabbage.

2 large duck breasts

honey marinade

1 tablespoon sesame oil

2 tablespoons soy sauce

1 tablespoon honey

1 teaspoon Tabasco sauce

orange salsa

1 shallot or small onion, finely chopped

2 oranges, segmented

1 yellow Scotch bonnet chile, or habanero, seeded and finely chopped

1 bunch of basil, roughly torn

1 small red bell pepper, seeded and finely chopped

sherry sauce

2 tablespoons dry sherry

⅔ cup vegetable stock

Serves 4

Harissa honey quail
roasted with sweet potatoes

Harissa paste is one of the great ingredients of North African and Middle Eastern cooking, and often served with dishes accompanied by couscous. It can be bought ready-made, but it is easy to make yourself— just soak 1 oz. dried chiles in warm water for 1 hour. Drain and puree with 2 tablespoons fresh cilantro, 1 tablespoon fresh mint, a pinch of salt, a garlic clove, and enough oil to produce a thick paste.

Mix the harissa and honey coating ingredients together, then spread onto the quail, place in a roasting pan and cook in a preheated oven at 400°F for about 20 minutes, or until tender. (The birds are cooked when a skewer inserted into the thickest part of the thigh produces clear juices with no trace of pink.) Set aside to rest for 10 minutes before serving. Cut the sweet potatoes into thick chunks, brush them with a little olive oil, sprinkle with sea salt, place in another roasting pan and cook at the same temperature for 20 minutes. Serve the quail with the sweet potatoes. A steamed green vegetable would be a suitable accompaniment.

4 quail

12 oz. sweet potatoes

2 teaspoons olive oil

sea salt

**harissa and
honey coating**

3 tablespoons honey

2 tablespoons
dry sherry

2 tablespoons
harissa paste

sea salt

Serves 4

Pan-fried venison
with chile and pear sauce

This delicious combination of fruit and meat is typical of Middle Eastern and medieval cookery. Add a dash of chile and soy sauce for an East-meets-West flavor. You could use venison sausages instead of venison for a simpler version of this recipe. If venison is unavailable use well-aged beef fillet instead.

Heat the butter and olive oil in a large skillet, add the venison and gently sauté for a few minutes until brown. Remove from the skillet and set aside to rest in a warm place.

Add the sliced pears to the skillet, sprinkle with the sugar, then gently sauté until lightly golden. Add the red wine, soy sauce, chile, and cornflour mixture, bring to a boil and simmer for 5 minutes. Serve the venison steaks with the sauce poured around, accompanied by steaming roast potatoes and shredded cabbage sautéed with caraway seeds. Alternatively, return the venison steaks to the sauce and simmer gently for 3 minutes before serving.

an unusual **sweet and spicy** dish

with just a hint of chile heat

2 tablespoons butter

1 tablespoon olive oil

1 lb. venison fillet
(or aged beef fillet),
cut into 1-inch steaks

2 pears, peeled,
quartered and sliced

½ teaspoon sugar

¾ cup red wine

1 tablespoon
light soy sauce

1 red chile, roasted

1 tablespoon
cornflour, mixed
with 2 tablespoons
cold water

Serves 4

Vegetables

Corn crêpes with
chile vegetables and tomato salsa

These pretty yellow pancakes, made with polenta, have a sweet, nutty texture. Add a dollop of sour cream and this dish could be served by itself for lunch, or as a appetizer — or as a sumptuous treat for vegetarians.

To make the crêpes, place the polenta grain, plain flour, and salt in a bowl, then beat in the eggs and milk to form a smooth batter. Set aside.
To make the filling, crush the garlic, slice the onions, and cut the squash in quarters. Core, seed and chop the red bell peppers and pickled chile.
Heat the oil in a skillet, add all the ingredients and sauté gently until just tender.
To make the salsa, roughly chop the tomatoes and finely chop the scallions. Seed and roughly chop the red chile, then mix all the filling ingredients together and chill until ready to use.
To cook the crêpes, heat the oil in a 7-inch skillet. Add a ladle of crêpe batter and swirl around so the mixture covers the base. Cook until the surface bubbles and the base is browned, then turn and brown the other side.
Remove and set aside in a warm place while you cook the remaining crêpes.
Spoon the filling into the crêpes and serve immediately with the tomato salsa.

½ cup polenta grain

½ cup plain flour

3 eggs

about 1 cup low-fat milk

pinch of salt

vegetable filling

2 garlic cloves

2 red onions

12 patty pan squash

2 red bell peppers

1 pickled red jalapeño chile

1 tablespoon olive oil

pinch of salt

2 tablespoons fresh cilantro

tomato salsa

4 ripe tomatoes

2 scallions

1 red chile

2 tablespoons red wine vinegar

Serves 4

Spinach dhaal
with toasted coconut

Lentils are a good source of protein for vegetarians and they work well as a base for hot chiles. In India, dhaal is a traditional accompaniment to rice, flat breads, curried vegetables, meats, or poultry.

Place the yellow split peas or channa dhaal in a saucepan, add the turmeric and about 4 cups water. Bring to a boil, then cover with the lid slightly ajar. Reduce the heat and simmer for about 20 minutes, then add salt and cook for about 15 to 20 minutes more, until the peas are cooked and tender, and have absorbed all the liquid. Heat the oil in a small skillet until very hot, add the cumin seeds, cinnamon, and chiles, and gently sauté to release the aromas. Add the spinach and sauté for a few minutes until the leaves turn bright green. Pile the spiced spinach on heated plates and spoon the yellow dhaal beside. Sprinkle with shredded coconut, if using, and serve.

12 oz. yellow split peas or channa dhaal, washed

½ teaspoon ground turmeric

1 teaspoon salt

3 tablespoons vegetable oil

1 teaspoon cumin seeds

1 cinnamon stick

3–5 dried, hot red chiles

8 oz. spinach leaves

2 tablespoons shredded coconut, or coconut flakes, toasted (optional), to serve

a **spicy trea**t for vegetarians—and great wit

eat and poultry

Provençal ragout
of tomatoes, fennel, and potato

A mild chile dish with just a hint of fire—
great for people with sensitive palates.

1 lb. tomatoes, peeled
and quartered

1 lb. new potatoes,
unpeeled

4 shallots

2 fennel bulbs,
trimmed and sliced

2 garlic cloves, crushed

1 red bell pepper

2 teaspoons harissa
paste (see page 39)

strip of orange peel

1 bay leaf

⅔ cup vegetable stock

2 tablespoons
sun-dried tomato pesto

2 red serrano chiles,
roasted and chopped

salt and freshly
ground black pepper

Serves 4

Place all the ingredients, except the sun-dried
tomato pesto and chiles, into a saucepan, bring to a
boil and simmer for 25 minutes.
Mix the sun-dried tomato pesto with the chiles, stir
into the stew and serve with crusty bread.

Caribbean curry

A mixture of pumpkin, plantains, bell peppers, and peas simmered in a chile and coconut stock, served with spiced rice. To make the rice, fry 1 teaspoon each of cinnamon, chopped ginger, and cumin seeds in 1 tablespoon of oil, then stir through plain boiled rice. If you can't find plantains, use bananas instead.

To prepare the butternut squash, cut in half, remove and discard the seeds, peel off the skin and cut the flesh into chunky cubes.

Heat the chile oil in a large saucepan, add the sliced chiles, cinnamon sticks, and cloves and let them sizzle to release their aromas.

Stir in the onions and cook until softened and a little golden. Stir in the squash and plantain, add the vegetable stock and coconut milk, bring to a boil and simmer for 10 minutes.

Add the pepper and peas, cook for a further 10 minutes and serve. Steaming spiced rice would be a suitable accompaniment.

2 butternut squash

1 tablespoon chile oil

2 red chiles, seeded and sliced

2 cinnamon sticks

6 cloves

1 onion, roughly chopped

1 plantain, peeled and thickly sliced

1¼ cups vegetable stock

⅔ cup coconut milk

1 teaspoon fresh lemon juice

1 green bell pepper, cored, seeded and cut into chunks

1 cup fresh or frozen peas

Serves 4

Rice noodles
with green papaya and daikon

Noodles served with a light sweet and sour sauce is a dish that's rapidly becoming the stir-fry of the nineties. This is delicious served with char-grilled beef, or as a fresh summer appetizer. Kaffir lime leaves are available at oriental markets, but grated lime zest could be used instead.

To make the chile dressing, mix together the lime juice, fish sauce, palm sugar, chiles, lime leaves, red shallots, and lemongrass. Set aside.
Cut the rice noodles into 6-inch strips, place in a colander, pour over a jug of boiling water and set aside. Peel and seed the papaya and cut into a fine julienne strips. Peel and slice the daikon.
Drain the softened noodles and place in a bowl. When cool, stir in the papaya, daikon, strips of chile, orange segments, and the dressing.
Serve, garnished with mint leaves.

8 oz. rice noodles

1 green papaya

1 daikon or mooli (Japanese radish)

2 red New Mexico chiles, cored, seeded, and cut into strips

1 orange, segmented

mint leaves, to serve

chile dressing

juice of 3 limes

4 tablespoons *nam pla* (Thai fish sauce)

4 teaspoons palm sugar

4 green chiles, seeded and finely sliced

4 small kaffir lime leaves, finely shredded

4 red shallots

3 stalks of fresh lemongrass, trimmed and thinly sliced

Serves 4

a modern update on a Thai recipe

with **five stars** on the chile heat scale

Vegetable fritters
with chile mint raita

Wonderful as party food, these light fritters
will also make perfect appetizers. Vary the
vegetables to suit yourself, and serve with
this wonderful raita with a hint of chile.

To make the raita, roughly chop the mint and
cilantro, and place in a mixing bowl. Seed and chop
the chiles. Peel and finely chop the ginger. Add to
the bowl with the garlic. Add the grated lime zest
and juice, together with the salt and yogurt.
Chill until ready to serve.
To make the spicy batter, first chop the fresh cilantro
and mint leaves, then place in a bowl with the flour,
turmeric, and sugar.
Whisk the egg white until stiff, carefully fold in the
spiced flour, stir in the lime juice, salt, and enough
water to give a light batter.
Break the cauliflower into flowerets, cut the zucchini
into 1-inch slices, and trim the carrots.
Heat vegetable oil in a deep-fryer or saucepan.
Dip each piece of vegetable into the batter and
deep-fry in hot oil until golden brown. Drain on
paper towels. Serve hot with the raita.

4 sprigs of cilantro

4 sprigs of mint

3 oz. gram flour

pinch of turmeric

pinch of sugar

1 egg white

juice of 1 lime

pinch of salt

8 oz. cauliflower

6 oz. zucchini

1 bunch of baby carrots

oil, for deep-frying

chile mint raita

4 sprigs of mint

4 sprigs of cilantro

2 green chiles

½ inch fresh ginger

1 garlic clove, crushed

2 limes

pinch of sea salt

4 tablespoons yogurt

Serves 4

Vegetable patties
with spicy tomato chutney

A great recipe for vegetarians—and equally
exciting for the rest of us!

1¼ lb. sweet potatoes

7 oz. carrots

12 oz. zucchini

1 green Asian chile

1 scallion

2 tablespoons yogurt

salt and black pepper

vegetable oil, for frying

**spicy tomato
chutney**

4 tomatoes

1–2 red chiles

2 tablespoons
chopped fresh mint

1 tablespoon
cider vinegar

pinch of sea salt

Serves 4

To make the chutney, roughly chop the tomatoes,
finely chop the chiles, then mix with the mint,
vinegar and salt. Set aside until ready to serve.
To make the patties, first boil and mash the sweet
potatoes. Trim and grate the zucchini, sprinkle with
salt, and set aside for 30 minutes to draw out some
of the juices. Drain and pat dry. Grate the carrots,
seed and chop the chile and slice the scallion.
Mix all the vegetables in a bowl, together with the
yogurt, salt, and pepper.
With floured hands, shape the mixture into 8 patties.
Heat a shallow layer of oil in a skillet and sauté the
patties for 4 minutes on both sides.
Serve immediately with the spicy tomato chutney.

Red pepper compote
with feta cheese

Olive oil is a great combo with chiles.

Roast, peel, seed, and quarter the bell peppers and chiles. Place a layer of peppers in a bowl, then a layer of feta. Season, add half the garlic and half a chile, then pour over some of the oil. Repeat until all ingredients have been used. Chill for 24 hours before serving with warmed bread and a selection of salads.

6 red bell peppers

2 red habanero or Scotch bonnet chiles

½ cup feta cheese

2 garlic cloves, crushed

1¼ cups olive oil

⅔ cup virgin olive oil

sea salt

Serves 4

Chile parsley pesto
for pasta and steamed vegetables

An especially zippy pesto—great with pasta, and terrific with bruschetta too.

To make the pesto, roast and peel the chiles and roast the pignoli nuts. Place all the ingredients in a blender or food processor and puree until smooth. Set aside until ready to use.
Trim and slice the leeks and cut the broccoli into flowerets. Cook the pasta in a pan of boiling salted water until just tender, and steam the vegetables. To serve, drain the pasta, place in a serving bowl or 4 heated pasta plates, stir in about 4 tablespoons of pesto, and pile the vegetables on top.

8 oz. leeks

8 oz. broccoli

1 lb. dried pasta

chile pesto

3 green caribe chiles

3 tablespoons pignoli nuts

1 small garlic clove

4 tablespoons olive oil

juice of 1 lime

1 bunch flat-leaf parsley

sea salt, to taste

Serves 4

Side dishes

Above, from left, Green chile paste (recipe page 61), Cucumber chile chutney (page 60), and Avocado relish (page 61).

Chile vodka

There are many wonderfully flavored vodkas—and parties to match! Your own fiery chile vodka will be a great conversation piece.

Add the chiles to the vodka and marinate for 1 to 2 days. Remove the chiles, keep the bottle in the freezer, and serve after dinner or as a nightcap after dancing the night away.

2 big red chiles or 4 smaller ones, halved lengthwise

1 bottle vodka

Makes 1 bottle

Chile chutney
with grapefruit and cucumber

This is an instant chutney best made and served within a few days. It is ideal for those lazy summer days full of convivial barbecue parties and general *al fresco* eating. Serve it with homemade burgers or sausages.

Peel the cucumbers, scoop out the seeds, slice, sprinkle over half the salt and leave to marinate while you prepare the remaining ingredients. Roughly chop the pickled cucumbers, finely dice the red onion, dice the tomatoes, shred the cabbage and seed and dice the chiles. Place all the vegetables in a bowl, squeeze over the citrus juices, sprinkle with salt, and stir well. Chill for up to 3 days before serving.

3 cucumbers

6 pickled dill cucumbers

2 red onions

1 lb. plum tomatoes

¼ white cabbage

2 serrano chiles, or 1 Thai

juice of 3 oranges

juice of ½ pink grapefruit

juice of 2 limes

1 tablespoon salt

Serves 8

Avocado relish

Avocados are packed with nutrients and their smooth, creamy texture is ideal for salsas.

Roast or broil the chiles and bell pepper, until the skins are blackened and blistered. Cover with plastic wrap for 3 to 5 minutes.
Remove and discard the skin, cores and seeds, then chop the flesh into small pieces.
Chop the avocado, brush with lemon juice and place in a bowl. Stir in the roasted pepper and chiles, add the scallions and cilantro and stir in the vinegar.
Serve as a relish or as a dip with tortillas.

2 green chiles

1 red bell pepper

2 ripe avocados, halved and peeled

juice of 1 lemon

4 scallions, finely chopped

1 large bunch of cilantro, roughly chopped

½ cup vinegar

Serves 4

Green chile paste

A mixture of fresh and roasted chiles makes a paste that's perfect when used like mustard with dishes such as roast chicken or grilled tuna steaks.

Roast or broil the Anaheim chiles until the skins are blackened and blistered. Place in plastic wrap for 3 to 5 minutes. Remove and discard the skins, cores, and seeds.
Place the flesh in a blender or food processor with the habaneros and garlic and puree to a paste.

4 Anaheim chiles

2 habanero chiles, cored and seeded

1 garlic clove, crushed

Makes one jar, about ½ cup

Green chile corn muffins
with chile and lime butter

Chili powder and fresh chiles give these
muffins lots of zing—for even more spice,
serve with this chile and lime butter. This is
a quick and easy recipe—just 10 minutes to
prepare and 12 to 15 minutes to cook.

To make the muffins, sift the flour, polenta, baking
powder, and chili powder together into a mixing
bowl. In a separate bowl, mix the milk, melted butter,
and beaten eggs, then fold into the dry mixture. Stir
in the grated orange rind and the chopped chiles.
Spoon the batter into a greased muffin pan and
bake in a preheated oven at 400°F for about
12 to 15 minutes until firm.
Remove and set aside on a wire rack.
To make the chile and lime butter, beat all the
ingredients together until soft and creamy.
Serve with the warm muffins.

2 cups plain flour

1½ cups fine polenta

3 teaspoons
baking powder

1 tablespoon
mild chili powder

¾ cup milk

6 tablespoons butter,
melted

2 eggs, lightly beaten

grated rind of 1 orange

2 green chiles,
seeded and chopped

**chile and
lime butter**

1 lime

4 tablespoons
(½ stick) butter

pinch of chili powder

Makes 12

chiles are a **surprising**, zippy

addition to these buttery yellow muffins

Index